HEMP JEWELRY

Written by Judy Ann Sadler
Illustrated by June Bradford

KIDS CAN PRESS

To Emily, a precious bead on my necklace of life — J.A.S.

To my very special niece Melanie, who has inspired me with her love
for life even through her continuing struggle with cystic fybrosis.
I love you Mel — we will always be together — J.B.

Text © 2005 Judy Ann Sadler
Illustrations © 2005 June Bradford

KIDS CAN DO IT and the logo are trademarks of Kids Can Press Ltd.

Kids Can Press acknowledges the financial support of the Government of Ontario,
through the Ontario Media Development Corporation's Ontario Book Initiative, and the
Government of Canada, through the BPIDP, for our publishing activity.

Published in Canada by
Kids Can Press Ltd.
29 Birch Avenue
Toronto, ON M4V 1E2

Published in the U.S. by
Kids Can Press Ltd.
2250 Military Road
Tonawanda, NY 14150

www.kidscanpress.com

Edited by Laurie Wark
Designed by Karen Powers and Sherill Chapman
Photography by Frank Baldassarra
Printed and bound in China

The hardcover edition of this book is smyth sewn casebound.
The paperback edition of this book is limp sewn with a drawn-on cover.

CM 05 0 9 8 7 6 5 4 3 2 1
CM PA 05 0 9 8 7 6 5 4 3 2 1

National Library of Canada Cataloguing in Publication Data

Sadler, Judy Ann, 1959–
Hemp jewelry / written by Judy Ann Sadler ; illustrated by June Bradford.

(Kids can do it)

ISBN 1-55337-774-5 (bound).   ISBN 1-55337-775-3 (pbk.)

1. Macramé — Juvenile literature. 2. Beadwork — Juvenile literature.
3. Jewelry making — Juvenile literature. I. Bradford, June II. Title. III. Series.

TT880.S24 2005   j746.42'22   C2004-903902-4

Kids Can Press is a lorus™ Entertainment company

Contents

Introduction

What happens when you cut some hemp, tie it in knots and add just the right beads? You get great hemp jewelry! Maybe you've seen colorful, beaded hemp bracelets at a store and wondered how they are made. Now you'll know! In this book you'll find all the information you need to make hemp bracelets, necklaces, anklets, rings and more. Once you've learned the basics of making hemp jewelry, you'll be able to combine knots and beads to create your own personal look. Get your friends together and show them how to make hemp jewelry, too!

MATERIALS

Hemp

Hemp cord is made from fiber found in the stalks of the tall, fast-growing hemp plant. It's especially good for making jewelry because hemp is strong, holds knots well and is soft enough to wear against your skin.

It usually comes in two sizes: 20 lb. and 48 lb. The number refers to its thickness: 20 lb. hemp is about 1 mm wide and 48 lb. hemp is about 2 mm wide. Both make great jewelry, but it is easier to thread beads onto 20 lb. hemp. Most of the projects in this book are made with 20 lb. hemp. Hemp is also available in a thinner cord suitable for more delicate jewelry.

Hemp is usually a natural, light tan color, but it also comes in colors such as bright yellow, denim blue and jet black. It is often uneven in places, but that is part of its earthy look.

Beads, charms and pendants

A fun part of creating hemp jewelry is finding just the right decorations to make your project perfect. Check craft-supply stores, specialty bead shops, bazaars and junk sales for glass, wood, ceramic, metal and acrylic beads, pendants and charms. It is easiest to thread beads with large holes, but if your beads have small holes, check page 22 for how to use them in your jewelry.

Clasps

Clasps are optional. It is best to use a ring and toggle or lobster claw clasp. See page 9 for how to fasten them on your jewelry.

Other supplies

You will also need scissors, a few medium and large safety pins, masking tape or other strong tape, buttons, fishing line, clear stretchy cord, small and large paper clips, a permanent marker and a ruler or measuring tape.

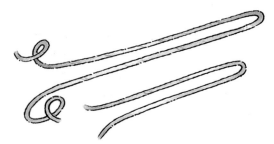

Great beginnings

The instructions for each project tell you how many pieces of hemp you will need and how long to cut them. You will usually use two hemp cords, one about three times longer than the other. It is best to unwind the cord end from inside the ball of hemp.

MAKING A STARTING LOOP

1. Fold each cord in half.

2. Hold the folded ends together and tie them in an overhand knot, leaving a small loop.

3. Pull each of the cords tight to make the knot smooth. (If you poke a pencil through the loop first, it will be easier to pull hard on each cord.)

4. The two short lengths of hemp are called the center cords, and the long ones are called the tying cords.

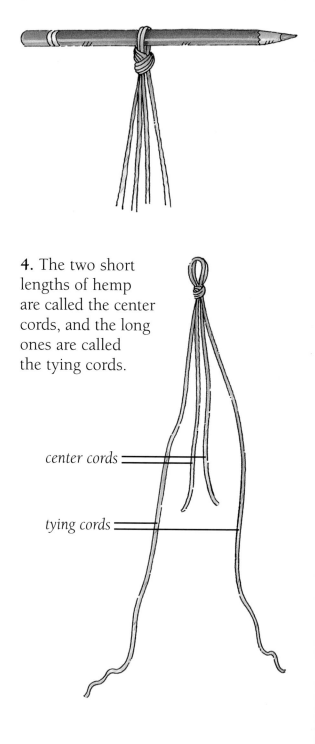

center cords

tying cords

Fastening the loop

You will need to hang, tape or pin your hemp in place. If the instructions don't suggest a fastening method, choose any method you like.

HANGING

Use masking tape to attach the starting loop and knot onto the edge of a table.

Overhand knot the center (short) cords together close to the ends. Pull apart a paper clip as shown, and hook it onto the center cords.

Hang a pair of scissors from the paper clip to weigh down the center cords and keep them straight as you knot.

TAPING

Use masking tape or other strong tape to hold down the starting loop and knot onto a table or other hard surface. Straighten the center cords and tape them down, too.

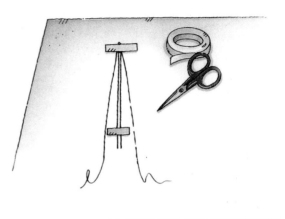

PINNING

Use a safety pin to fasten the starting loop to your bed, a pillow, a carpet, your jeans or another soft surface. Make a loose knot in the center cords and pin them down, too.

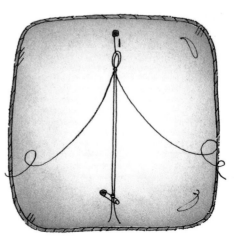

Happy endings

You can fasten your finished hemp jewelry with a bead, button, knot or clasp, or simply tie the ends together.

BEAD OR BUTTON

The bead or button you use should fit snugly through the loop so your jewelry doesn't come undone. If you use a button, it should be a shank button, the kind with a loop on the back.

1. Thread all the hemp cords through the bead or button. (If they don't all fit, thread two of them, then knot and trim the others short.)

2. Use an overhand knot to tie the cords together. Trim the ends short.

3. Push the bead or button through the starting loop.

KNOT

This method works best if the starting loop is small.

1. Gather the cord ends together and tie them in an overhand knot. Trim the ends short.

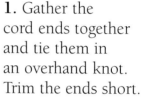

2. Push the knot through the loop — it should be a tight fit.

CLASP

You must attach part of the clasp before you start knotting. If possible, fasten both parts of the clasp together so that you don't lose the second part of the clasp.

1. After you have measured and cut your hemp, thread the clasp onto the middle of both cords. If it doesn't fit, thread it onto just the short cord.

2. Fold the cords in half, and tie them in an overhand knot very close to the end with the clasp inside the small loop.

3. When you are finished making your piece of jewelry, slide the second part of the clasp onto one or more of the cords. Tie all the cords together with an overhand knot. Trim the ends short.

TYING

You can simply tie the ends of your jewelry together if you don't mind not being able to take it off or if it is large enough to slide off without being undone.

1. Thread half the hemp cords through the starting loop.

2. Gather all the cords and tie them together with an overhand knot. Trim the ends short.

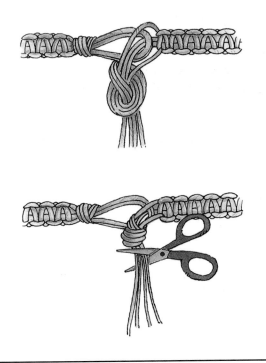

Spiral bracelet

This simple half-knot creates a beautiful spiral pattern. See page 13 for how to add beads to spiral jewelry.

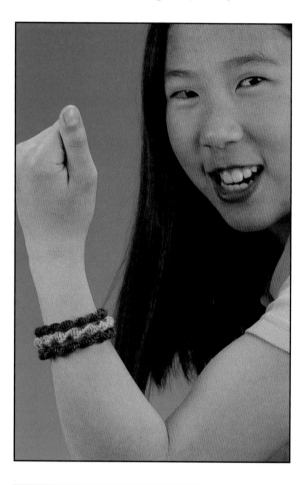

YOU WILL NEED

- a piece of hemp 90 cm (36 in.) long
- a piece of hemp 230 cm (90 in.) long
- a ruler or measuring tape, scissors, masking tape, a large paper clip

1   Make a starting loop (page 6). Fasten your hemp in place using the hanging method (page 7).

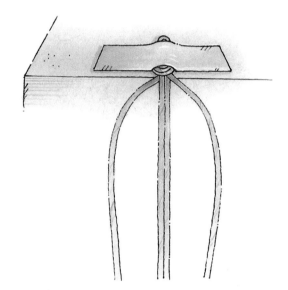

2   Bring the left tying cord across the center cords and behind the right tying cord. This forms a half-circle shape on the left side.

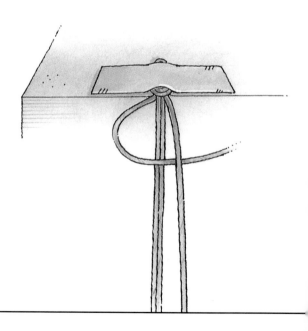

3 Bring the right cord behind the center cords and pull it through the half circle on the left.

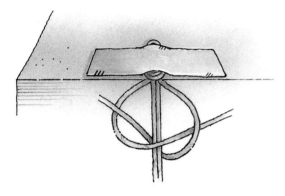

4 Pull both tying cords so the knot moves up the center cords to the overhand knot at the top of the bracelet. Now pull the cords firmly so the knot is tight. You have just completed a half-knot.

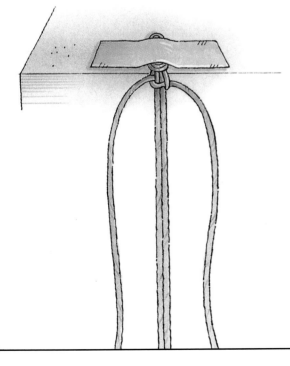

5 Keep making half-knots by repeating steps 2–4, always starting with the cord on the left. Allow the cords to spiral and change sides every few knots.

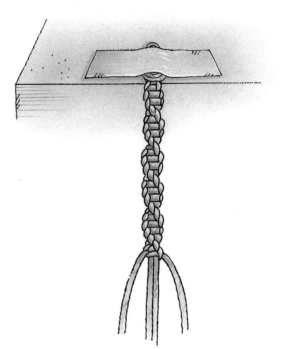

6 When your bracelet is the right length, see pages 8–9 for how to finish it.

Spiral pendant necklace

Find a special pendant or charm to use on this necklace. See page 13 for how to add beads to spiral jewelry.

YOU WILL NEED

- a piece of hemp 1.5 m (5 ft.) long
- a piece of hemp 5.5 m (18 ft.) long
  - a pendant or charm
  - 3 small rubber bands
- a ruler or measuring tape, scissors, masking tape, a large paper clip

1 Make a starting loop (page 6). Fasten your hemp in place using the hanging method (page 7).

2 Bundle each tying cord by winding it in a figure 8 pattern between your index and middle fingers. Fasten each bundle with a rubber band. Bundle the extra length on the center cords, too, and fasten them together with a rubber band. Pull out cord as you need it.

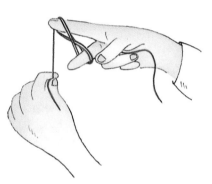

3 Make half-knots (steps 2–5, pages 10–11) until your necklace is half the length you'd like it to be (you may want to hold it up to your neck). Undo one of the bundles of tying cord and thread the cord through the pendant or charm. Continue knotting your necklace.

4 When your necklace is the right length, see pages 8–9 for how to finish it.

Beaded spiral jewelry

Add pizzazz to your spiral bracelet or necklace with a colorful batch of beads with large holes.

1 After knotting about 1 cm (½ in.) of the bracelet from pages 10–11, or about 5 cm (2 in.) of the necklace from page 12, remove the scissors and paper clip from the center cords.

2 Undo or snip off the knot in the center cords and thread on beads in the order you'd like them to be on your jewelry. Re-knot the cords and hang up the scissors.

3 Slide up a bead to the knotted part of the jewelry. Make more half-knots, then slide up another bead. Continue in this way.

4 When your jewelry is the right length, see pages 8–9 for how to finish it.

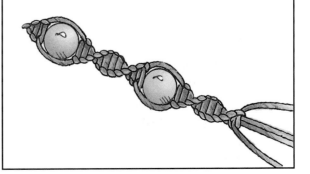

Square-knot bracelet

You will use this square knot often when making hemp jewelry. See page 16 for how to add beads to this bracelet.

YOU WILL NEED

- a piece of hemp 90 cm (36 in.) long
- a piece of hemp 230 cm (90 in.) long
- a permanent marker
- a ruler or measuring tape, scissors, a large paper clip, masking tape

---

1 Make a starting loop (page 6) and set up your hemp (page 7).

2 Mark the left tying cord by coloring the end with a marker or by wrapping a small piece of tape around it.

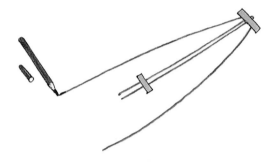

3 Bring the marked cord across the center cords and behind the right cord. This forms a half circle on the left side.

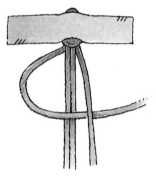

4 Bring the right cord behind the center cords and pull it through the half circle on the left.

5 Pull both cords so the knot moves up the center cords to the overhand knot. Pull firmly on the cords so the knot is tight.

6 Bring the marked cord, now on the right side, across the center cords and behind the left cord. This forms a half circle on the right side.

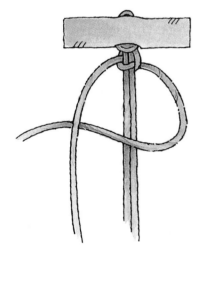

7 Bring the left cord behind the center cords and pull it through the half circle on the right. Pull both cords so the knot moves up the center cords to the overhand knot. Pull firmly on the cords so the knot is tight. This completes a square knot.

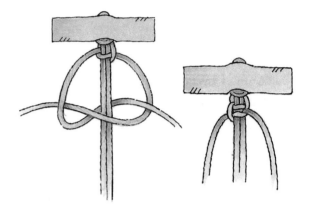

8 Keep making square knots by repeating steps 3–7, always starting with the marked cord, until your bracelet is the right length. See pages 8–9 for how to finish it.

Beaded square-knot bracelet

Choose a few colorful beads with large holes to jazz up your bracelet.

YOU WILL NEED

- materials for the square-knot bracelet on page 14
- a few beads with large holes

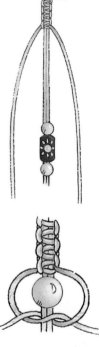

1 Knot the bracelet from page 14 until it is at least 1 cm (½ in.) long and the marked cord is on the left side.

2 Unfasten the center cords and thread on your beads in the order you'd like them to be on your bracelet.

3 Slide up a bead to the knots. Make more square knots, then slide up another bead. Continue in this way, with the marked cord always on the left before you add another bead.

4 When your bracelet is the right length, see pages 8–9 for how to finish it.

Beaded square-knot necklace

This necklace also looks great with a large bead in the center.

YOU WILL NEED

- a piece of hemp 120 cm (48 in.) long
- a piece of hemp 5 m (16 ft.) long
- beads with large holes
- 3 small rubber bands
- a permanent marker
- a ruler or measuring tape, scissors, a large paper clip, masking tape

1 Make a starting loop (page 6), then thread beads onto the center cords in the order you'd like them to be on your necklace.

2 Set up your hemp (page 7), then bundle the extra lengths of cord (step 2, page 12).

3 Make about 5 cm (2 in.) of square knots (steps 2–7, pages 14–15) until the marked cord is on the left side. Slide up a bead to the knots. Make more square knots, then slide up another bead. Continue in this way, with the marked cord always on the left before you add another bead.

4 When your necklace is the right length, see pages 8–9 for how to finish it.

Mixed-up anklet

You can also mix up the colors of your tying and center cords, then combine half-knots and square knots. Try this for a bracelet and necklace, too!

YOU WILL NEED

- 2 different-colored pieces of hemp, each 230 cm (90 in.) long
- a permanent marker
- a ruler or measuring tape, scissors, masking tape, a large paper clip

1 Fold the cords about 50 cm (20 in.) from the end. Tie them together in an overhand knot, leaving a small loop. Pull each of the cords tightly to make the knot smooth.

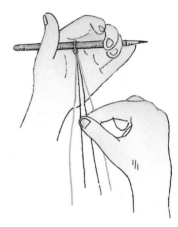

2 Separate the cords so the short cords (one of each color) are in the center. Fasten your hemp in place using the hanging method (page 7).

3 Make about 2.5 cm (1 in.) of square knots (steps 2–7, pages 14–15).

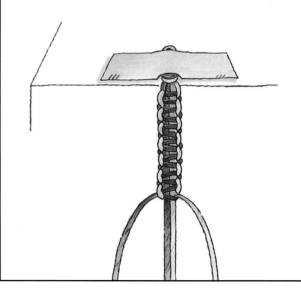

4 Make about 2.5 cm (1 in.) of half-knots (steps 2–5, pages 10–11). Begin each knot with the cord on the left side (you will be alternating colors) and allow your hemp to turn as you knot.

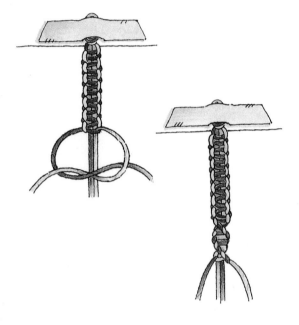

MORE IDEAS

• Thread on beads before you knot the center cords together. Alternate square and half-knots, sliding up a bead whenever you like. If you need more beads, undo or snip off the knot in the center cords, thread on more beads and continue.

• Make this anklet in just one color of hemp. The pattern of square knots and spirals will show up clearly.

5 Go back to making square knots. Keep alternating knots until your anklet is the right length. See pages 8–9 for how to finish it.

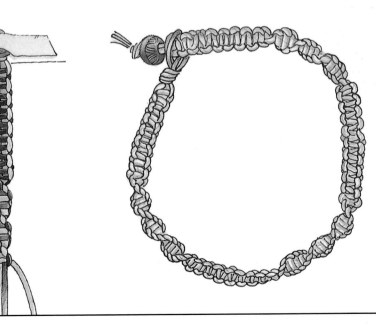

Switcheroo anklet

This interesting pattern is quick to knot and doesn't use much hemp. Try it with two different colors if you like.

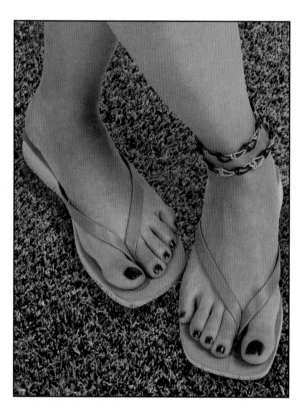

YOU WILL NEED

- 2 pieces of hemp, each 120 cm (48 in.) long
- a permanent marker
- a ruler or measuring tape, scissors, masking tape

1 Make a starting loop (page 6), then tape the hemp to your work surface. Don't fasten the center cords because they will be switching places with the tying cords.

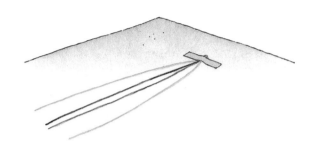

2 Make one square knot (steps 2–7, pages 14–15). Since the center cords aren't fastened down, you will need to hold them together and pull lightly as you knot.

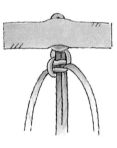

3 Bring the tying cords together in the center. Make the old center cords the new tying cords. Mark the cord on the left with the marker. Whenever you switch the cords, position the marked cords on the left.

4 Make another square knot, but instead of tightening it against the first knot, leave a space of about 1 cm (½ in.) and tighten it there.

5 Continue in this way, switching the center and tying cords after each square knot.

6 When your anklet is the right length, see pages 8–9 for how to finish it.

MORE IDEAS

• Thread a small bead onto each tying cord and medium beads onto both center cords, or thread large beads onto all the cords at any point.

• Use three different colors of hemp, each 120 cm (48 in.) in length. Tie them together with an overhand knot. Make a square knot using the two cords of one color for the tying cords while holding the other four cords in the center. For the second square knot, use one of the center colors for the tying cords. For the third square knot, use the last color. Repeat the pattern until your anklet is the right length.

Any-bead bracelet

You can add beads with very small holes to your hemp jewelry. The trick is to use fishing line or beading thread for the center cords.

YOU WILL NEED

- a piece of fishing line 90 cm (36 in.) long
- a piece of hemp 230 cm (90 in.) long
- 10 to 20 beads with small holes
- a permanent marker
- a ruler or measuring tape, scissors, a large paper clip, masking tape

1 Fold the fishing line and hemp in half and make a starting loop (page 6).

2 Fasten your hemp (page 7), but thread on your beads before you knot the center fishing lines together. Thread on the beads in the order you'd like them to be on your bracelet.

3 Make about 1 cm (½ in.) of square knots (steps 2–7, pages 14–15). Keep the knots tight so you can't see the fishing line in the center.

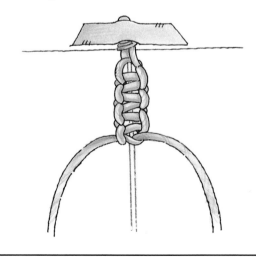

4 With the marked cord on the left, slide a bead up the fishing line to the knots. Make more square knots, then slide up another bead. Always finish a square knot before you add another bead or your bracelet will start to twist.

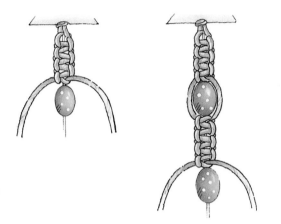

5 Keep knotting and adding beads. If you need more beads, undo or snip off the knot in the fishing line, thread on more beads and continue.

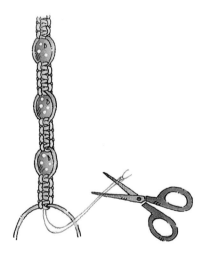

6 When your bracelet is the right length, see pages 8–9 for how to finish it.

MORE IDEAS

● Make a bracelet or necklace that is more beads than knots. Start with at least one square knot, slide up a bead, make another square knot and slide up another bead. Continue this pattern of one bead to one knot and you'll soon have a gorgeous beaded bracelet or necklace. Try this with fine hemp, too, for a more delicate look.

Loopy bracelet

This lovely bracelet is made using a knot called a double half hitch. Make it in any combination of colors. These measurements are suitable for an anklet, too.

YOU WILL NEED

- 2 different-colored pieces of hemp, each 150 cm (60 in.) long

- a ruler or measuring tape, scissors, a large paper clip, masking tape

1 Fold the cords about 40 cm (16 in.) from the end. Tie them together in an overhand knot, leaving a small loop. Separate the cords so the short cords, one of each color, are in the center, then fasten your hemp (page 7).

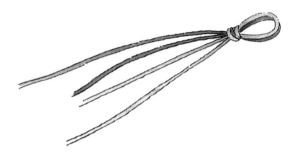

2 Bring the left tying cord across and around the center cords, and pull it through the half circle formed on the left.

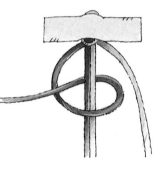

3 Pull the left tying cord so the loop moves up the center cords to the overhand knot. Pull the cord firmly so the knot is tight.

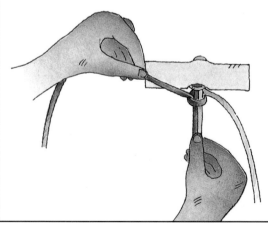

4 Repeat steps 2–3. This completes a double half hitch.

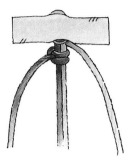

5 Make a double half hitch on the right side with the right tying cord, but before you tighten the knot, leave a small loop.

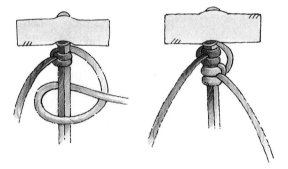

6 Keep knotting this way, on one side and then the other, leaving loops as you go.

7 When your bracelet is the right length, see pages 8–9 for how to finish it.

MORE IDEAS

• Thread beads onto the center cords or onto one or both tying cords whenever you like. You can also thread charms onto the tying cords of this bracelet.

• Rather than leaving loops on each side of this bracelet, pull the knots tight. You will get a narrower, zipper-like pattern.

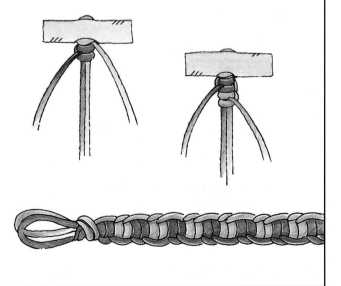

Daisy-chain choker

The instructions for this charming choker use pink, yellow and green beads, but you can substitute any colors you want.

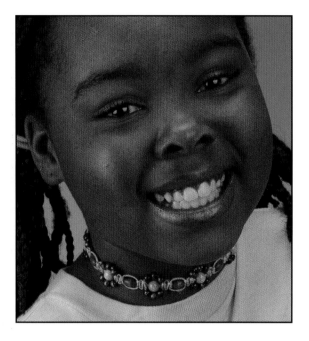

YOU WILL NEED

- a piece of hemp 150 cm (60 in.) long
- a piece of hemp 3 m (9 ft.) long
- about 60 small pink beads
- about 11 small-to-medium green beads
- about 10 small-to-medium yellow beads
- a permanent marker
- a ruler or measuring tape, scissors, a large paper clip, masking tape

1 Make a starting loop (page 6), then alternate threading the green and yellow beads onto the center cords, starting and ending with green beads. Fasten your hemp (page 7).

2 Make four square knots (steps 2–7, pages 14–15), then slide up a green bead. Make two more square knots.

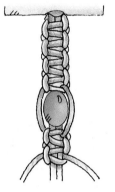

3 Thread three pink beads onto each tying cord. (If the hemp frays, wet and pinch the end together or trim it and try again.)

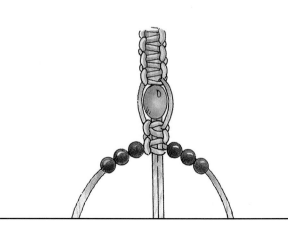

4 Slide up a yellow bead. Position the six pink beads around the yellow flower center.

6 Slide up a green bead, make two more square knots and make another flower.

7 Continue this pattern until you have made about eight flowers. Try on the choker to see if you need more flowers and knots.

5 Make two more square knots. Always start the square knots with the marked cord on the left so the choker does not twist.

8 When your choker is the right length, remove any extra beads. See pages 8–9 for how to finish it.

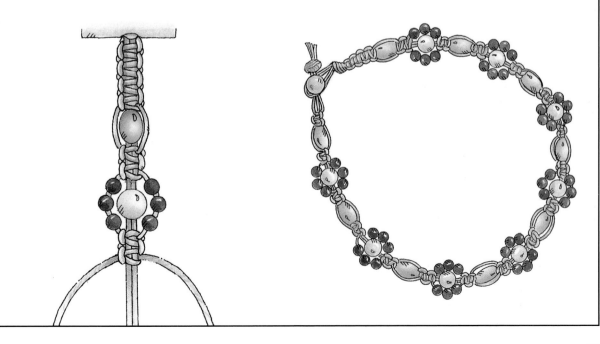

Lacy choker

This lacy choker pattern makes
a nice wide bracelet, too.

YOU WILL NEED

- 4 pieces of hemp, each 250 cm (100 in.) long
- 5 to 7 medium beads with large holes
- a ruler or measuring tape, scissors, masking tape

---

1 Hold all four cords together, fold them in half and make a starting loop (page 6). Tape down the loop.

2 Choose four center cords to make a square knot (steps 3–7, pages 14–15).

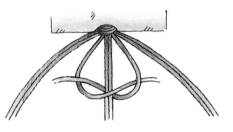

3 Make another square knot using the four cords on the left. Two of the cords will be from the center knot. Position the new knot to the left of and below the first knot.

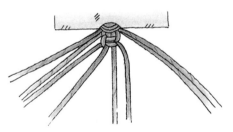

4 Make a square knot with the four cords on the right. Two of the cords will be the other cords from the center knot. Position the new knot to the right of and below the center knot.

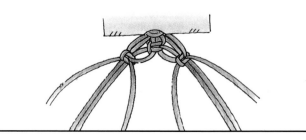

5 Make another square knot in the center, one on the left side and one on the right side. Leave space between each knot so the pattern looks lacy.

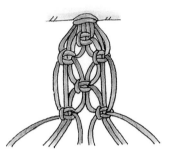

6 Continue this pattern until you've knotted about 5 cm (2 in.). Thread a bead onto the two center cords, then make knots on the left side, on the right side and in the center.

7 Knot the next 18–20 cm (7–8 in.) this way: Make a knot on the left side and on the right side, then thread a bead up the center; make a knot on the left side, on the right side and in the center.

8 End the choker the same way you began: a knot on the left side, on the right side and in the center, no beads.

9 When your choker is the right length, see pages 8–9 for how to finish it.

MORE IDEAS

• Instead of threading beads onto the center cords, thread smaller beads onto some or all of the tying cords, or onto the tying cords and center cords.

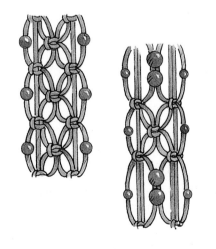

Knotty pendant necklace

Use a special chunky bead, pendant or charm on this unique necklace.

YOU WILL NEED

- 2 pieces of hemp, each 150 cm (60 in.) long
- 2 pieces of hemp, each 120 cm (48 in.) long
- a large bead, pendant or charm
- 9 small beads
- a ruler or measuring tape, scissors, a large paper clip, masking tape

1 Center your bead or pendant on one of the 150 cm (60 in.) pieces of hemp. Make an overhand knot, leaving a small space between the knot and the bead. Tape the bead onto your work surface.

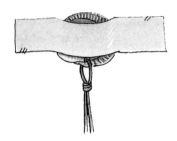

2 Thread the other 150 cm (60 in.) piece of hemp through the space between the knot and the bead. Bring the ends together to make them even.

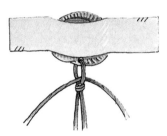

3 Make a square knot (steps 3–7, pages 14–15) using the second piece of hemp for the center cords.

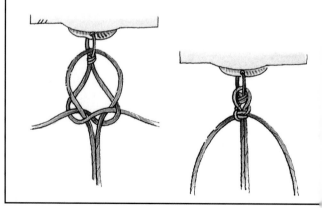

4 Thread a small bead onto each tying cord, then make another square knot.

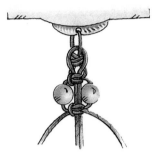

5 Switch the positions of the tying cords and the center cords, then make another square knot. Leave a space of about 1 cm (1/2 in.) and tighten the knot there.

6 Thread a bead onto the center cords, then switch and use the center cords as the tying cords for the next square knot. Switch the cords again for another square knot.

7 You have finished knotting the stem of the Y shape. Separate the four cords so you have a tying cord and a center cord on the left, and a center cord and a tying cord on the right.

8 Hold the two 120 cm (48 in.) pieces of hemp together. Match their centers to the fork of the Y. On the right side of the fork, paper clip the two new cords to the cords already there.

9 On the left side, use the new cords as the center cords and make two square knots.

Instructions continue on the next page ☞

10 Remove the paper clip from the other side and make two square knots.

11 Remove the tape from the large bead and reposition the necklace so the bead is straight out to the left. Fasten the necklace by taping across the square knots you just made.

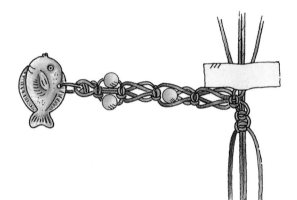

12 You will now knot one side of the necklace. Thread a bead onto the center cords, then use them as the tying cords for a square knot.

13 Make three more square knots, switching the positions of the cords each time and leaving space between each knot.

14 Thread on another bead, then make four more switched-around square knots. Thread on another bead and make switched-around square knots until you have a total of about 18 cm (7 in.) of knots.

15 Repeat steps 12–14 on the other side.

16 Try on the necklace. If you need more knots, add the same number to each side to keep the necklace balanced.

17 To create a fastening loop, tie an overhand knot at one end, leave a space of about 1 cm (½ in.) and then tie another overhand knot. See pages 8–9 for how to finish your necklace.

MORE IDEAS

● Use any combination of knots and beads for this necklace. Or use two different colors of hemp. Or make the whole necklace in a spiral pattern with half-knots (steps 2–5, pages 10–11).

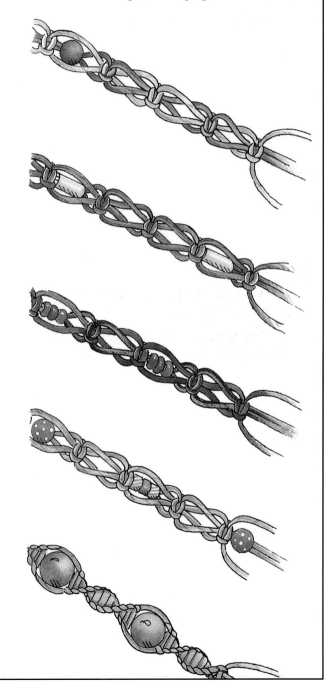

Time for hemp

Do you have a watch with a broken or boring band? Make a knotty new band from hemp and beads that match your watch face, or choose whatever colors you like.

YOU WILL NEED

- 8 pieces of hemp, each 60 cm (24 in.) long
- a wristwatch with the band removed
- small beads with large holes
- a medium shank button
- a ruler or measuring tape, scissors, masking tape

---

1 Fold one of the cords in half. Push the looped end through the space between the watch face and the band bar. Pull the cord ends through the loop and pull until the hemp is fastened tightly to the bar. This is a lark's head knot.

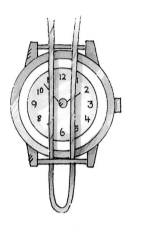 

2 Use the lark's head knot to fasten the other three cords beside the first one, then attach four cords to the other side of the watch the same way.

3 Tape the cords on one side of the watch to your work surface.

4 Make a square knot (steps 3–7, pages 14–15) using the four center cords.

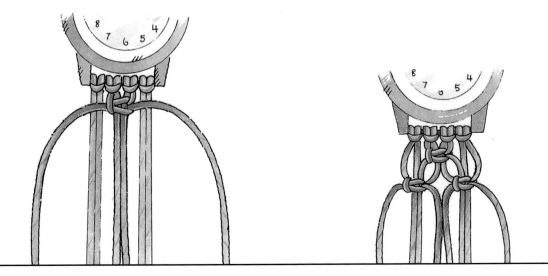

5 Make another square knot using the four cords on the left. Two of the cords will be from the center knot. Position the new knot to the left of and below the first knot.

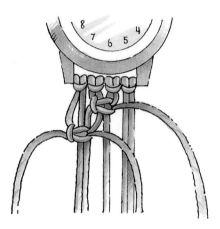

6 Make a square knot with the four cords on the right. Two of the cords will be the other cords from the center knot. Position the new knot to the right of and below the center knot. Leave space between each knot so the pattern looks lacy.

Instructions continue on the next page ☞

7 Make another square knot in the center. Thread a bead onto the far left and the far right cords, then tie square knots on the left and right sides.

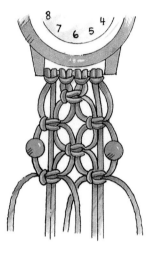

8 Thread a bead onto both the center cords together or thread one or two small beads onto each of the center cords separately, then make a square knot. Continue knotting and beading until you have about 5 cm (2 in.), ending with a knot on the left and right but not in the center.

9 Remove the tape from the unknotted end, tape down the knotted end and repeat steps 4–8.

10 Try on the watch. If the band is too small, make a few more knots. If it is almost the right length, you are ready to finish it.

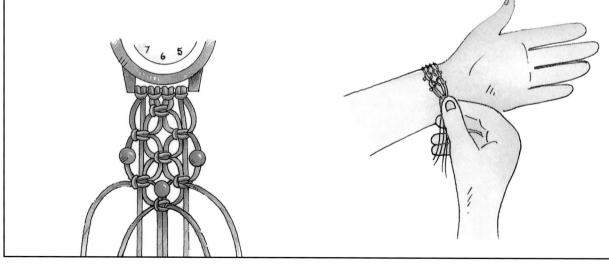

11 Tape down one end of the watch. On the opposite end, make a square knot with four cords in the center and two tying threads on each side. This brings together all the cords and leaves a small hole in the center of the band. Make an overhand knot with all eight cords, then trim the ends short.

13 Make another square knot with four cords in the center and two tying threads on each side. Make an overhand knot with all eight cords, then trim the ends short.

14 Fasten the watch by pushing the button through the hole in the opposite side.

12 Remove the tape, then tape down the finished end. On the opposite end, thread the shank button onto the two center cords, then make a square knot.

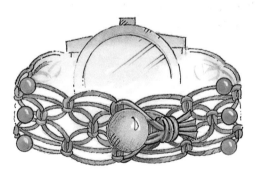

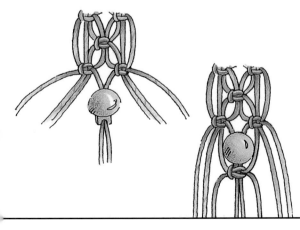

Knotty earrings

Thin hemp is ideal for earrings,
but any hemp will do.

YOU WILL NEED

- 2 pieces of hemp, each 50 cm (20 in.) long
- beads
- 2 earring hoops or wires
- a permanent marker
- a ruler or measuring tape, scissors, masking tape

1 Fold each cord in half and tie them in an overhand knot, leaving a tiny loop. Finish setting up your hemp (page 7).

2 Knot the hemp using half-knots (steps 2–5, pages 10–11), square knots (steps 2–7, pages 14 – 15), or other combinations of knots and beads from projects in this book.

3 Finish by tying the four cords in an overhand knot and trimming the ends short.

4 Hang the earring on a hoop or wire and make another one.

Rings on your fingers and toes

Combine some scraps of hemp with beads and clear, stretchy cord and you've got an easy-to-make ring. The stretchy cord makes the ring easy to put on and comfortable to wear.

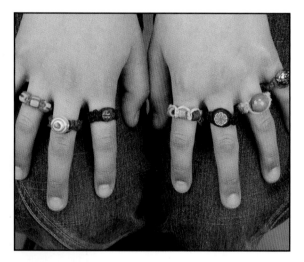

YOU WILL NEED

- a piece of hemp 70 cm (28 in.) long
- a piece of clear, stretchy cord 30 cm (12 in.) long (available at craft-supply stores)
- beads
- a permanent marker
- a ruler or measuring tape, scissors, masking tape

1 Fold the hemp and stretchy cord in half, then make a tiny starting loop (page 6) and set up your cords (page 7).

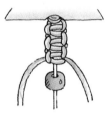

2 Make a few square knots (steps 2–7, pages 14–15), keeping the stretchy cords in the center. Thread a bead or two onto the center cords and make more square knots.

3 When your ring is the right size, thread one of the stretchy cord ends through its starting loop. Tie the stretchy cord ends in a tight overhand knot and trim them short.

4 Tie the hemp ends into an overhand knot, too, and trim them short.